Tony Buzan and Richard Israel

Cartoons by Dru Fuller

Gower

Published by
Gower Publishing Limited
Gower House
Croft Road
Aldershot
Hampshire GU11 3HR
England

Gower
Old Post Road
Brookfield
Vermont 05036
USA

Tony Buzan and Richard Israel have asserted their right under the Copyright, Designs and Patents Act 1988 to be identified as the authors of this work.

Mind Maps® Registered Trade Mark Buzan Organisation Ltd.
Inner Modelling® Registered Trade Mark Inner Modelling Inc.

British Library Cataloguing in Publication Data

Buzan, Tony
   Supersellf
   1. Selling – Psychological aspects
   I. Title II. Israel, Richard, 1942– III. Fuller, Dru
   658.8′5

ISBN 0 566 07887 2

Printed in Great Britain by Hartnolls Ltd, Bodmin.

Contents

v

Preface

Every sale starts in your head. So, the more you understand your sales brain, the better your sales results. It's as easy as that!

Our book *Brain Sell* started with this revelation. Within a month of publication a reader, Ian Broderick, wrote to us. Ian, a hairdresser living in Plumstead, London, had read *Brain Sell*, applied it, and increased his commission on hair product sales from £50 to £450 a week!

We were thrilled – not only by Ian's sales success, but also with the ease with which he had achieved higher sales. In fact, in his letter Ian mentioned that thousands of other hair stylists could do the same. For his success wasn't due to lots of complex knowledge, but rather the simple application of whole-brain selling.

Such instances of success inspired us to develop a quick, easy format for all readers. "How about a comic?" we thought. It's quick and fun to read, and could reveal the key Brain Sell concepts by means of an adventure story and personal exercises to advance your selling ability.

Gower, our publisher, encouraged us and the result is in your hands. *SuperSellf* is written in two parts. Part One "The Big Adventure" contains 14 exciting stories about Bob, Sue and SuperSellf, the stars of our comic. Exercises follow each story and we strongly recommend that you do them. Why? Because there is a SuperSellf inside you, just waiting to get out, and these exercises are designed to release it.

Part Two "Brain Train" is a complete 30-day mental workout. The special whole-brain exercises featured here come with a comprehensive 30-page Brain Train Diary so that you can track your progress. Now, in just minutes each day, you can get your sales brain into shape and enjoy all the benefits of whole-brain fitness!

Please send us your SuperSellf success stories so that we can include them in future materials. Write to us at SuperSellf, 54 Parkstone Road, Poole, Dorset BH15 2PX or e-mail: Buzan_Centres_Ltd@ compuserve.com.

Tony Buzan
Richard Israel

Introduction

I'M **TONY BUZAN**. WELCOME TO OUR *ADVENTURE STORY.*

SuperSelf

COME, BOB, I WANT TO SHOW YOU SOMETHING!

AN *ADVENTURE* IN TWO PARTS,

and I'M **RICHARD ISRAEL.**

PART ONE IS THE STORY OF A YOUNG MARRIED COUPLE, BOB and SUE.

BIO

BOB SELLS INDUSTRIAL PROPERTIES at ACE SALES.

SUE SELLS COSMETICS AT A DEPARTMENT STORE.

BOB FINDS SELLING MORE DIFFICULT THAN HE THOUGHT.

AND DOESN'T KNOW THAT IT'S HIS WAY OF THINKING THAT'S HOLDING HIM BACK.

SUE IS NEW TO SELLING COSMETICS.

SHE'S EAGER TO LEARN and HAS AN OPEN MIND.

1

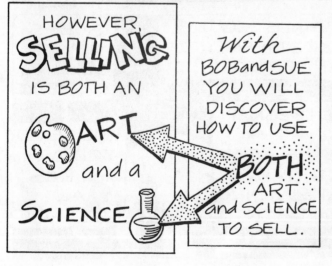

2

YOUR PERSONAL BRAIN TRAINER *SUPERSELLF* WILL TAKE YOU THROUGH YOUR **MENTAL FITNESS** PROGRAMME WHICH INCLUDES...

The Brain Train Diary

- SPECIAL MENTAL EXERCISES
- DAILY DIARY
- RECORD KEEPING PAGES

YOU BECOME THE HERO AS YOU DISCOVER HOW TO EVOLVE INTO A *SUPERSELLF* IN JUST 30 DAYS.

MEET DRU, OUR ARTIST, WHO ILLUSTRATED THE STORY.

I HAD SO MUCH FUN DOING IT!

AND YOU'LL HAVE SO MUCH **FUN** IN THE FOLLOWING PAGES *AS YOU DISCOVER*

YOUR *Supersellf!*

PART ONE — THE BIG ADVENTURE

1
YOU and your Superself

THE DAY BEGINS AT ACE PROPERTIES

BOB, THE BOSS WANTS TO SEE YOU RIGHT NOW!

SALES

GOOD MORNING, SIR!

GET YOUR ACT TOGETHER OR ELSE!

WHY DON'T MY CUSTOMERS BELIEVE ME?

I JUST CAN'T SELL.

I HATE MY JOB!

MY MEMORY IS SO BAD!

Antiques

OPEN

WHAT A LOSER!

8

LITTLE DID BOB REALIZE THAT HIS LIFE WAS ABOUT TO CHANGE... *Forever*!

HELLO, BOB

YES, BOB, I AM YOUR *SUPERSELLF*.

I'M GOING TO TEACH YOU and SUE EVERYTHING YOU NEED TO KNOW TO GET YOUR SALES MOVING!

BOB DISCOVERS HIS *SUPERSELLF*, AND OUR ADVENTURE BEGINS.

HAVE I FOUND THE FORMULA FOR SUCCESSFUL SELLING?

HE RUSHES HOME TO GIVE SUE HER GIFT.

Remember, Reader, THERE IS A *SUPERSELLF* INSIDE YOU JUST WAITING TO GET OUT.

9

EXERCISE 1

You and Your SuperSellf

In the Introduction you were introduced to Bob's SuperSellf. Each of us has a SuperSellf waiting to boost our sales.

The following exercises will help you contact your SuperSellf.

On a sheet of clean paper write the heading "I can improve my sales by ..." then list all the ideas you can think of. Take your time. When you have completely exhausted all the ideas place the page in a safe place for future reference. Do this now before reading any further.

Now, for the next ten minutes, do something completely different – take a walk, read the paper, listen to the radio.

Then, take a fresh sheet of paper and, without referring to your first list of answers, write "I can improve my sales by ..." and list all the ideas you can think of, but this time with your non-dominant hand (this is the hand you don't normally write with, so if you are right-handed use your left hand and vice versa). Take your time. Notice how it feels to use your non-dominant hand. Because each hand is controlled by a different side of the brain, using your non-dominant hand will allow you to tap into the often underutilized side and a new way of thinking.

When you have completed the second page, compare it to the first page. What conclusions can you reach? Are both pages the same or have you discovered a new part of yourself?

Do this exercise every few weeks. You can change the statements.

- "I can find new customers by ..."
- "I can improve my selling skills by ..."
- "I can develop my product knowledge by ..."
- "I can improve my customer care skills by ..."
- "I can add value to my customer by ..."

Make up your own statements.

Save all your answers for future reference. As the months progress and you repeat this exercise, you will be pleased that you have earlier answers to reflect back on.

Trigger Fingers

HOW TO TURN BRAIN CELLS *into* BRAIN SELLS.

LET'S SURF SUE'S BRAIN WAVES.

THIS IS WHAT'S INSIDE ALL OUR HEADS, OUR BIO COMPUTER BRAIN WITH DIFFERENT MENTAL PROGRAMMES.

NUMBERS

WORDS

LOGIC

LISTS

DETAILS

THESE ARE THE FIRST 5 PROGRAMMES.

NUMBERS

NUMBERS ALLOW US TO +, −, × and ÷.

WE USE **WORDS** TO COMMUNICATE.

LOGIC TO MAKE THE SALE.

CLOSING
OVERCOME OBJECTIONS
PRESENTING
QUALIFYING
GREETING

TOP 10 HITS OF THE WEEK

LISTS TO GIVE ORDER AND PRIORITY.

TO DO
☑ CALL ON TUES.
☑ PREFERS RED
☑ BIRTHDAY ON 26TH
☐ NEED TAX INFO FOR LOAN

DETAILS TO PULL IT ALL TOGETHER.

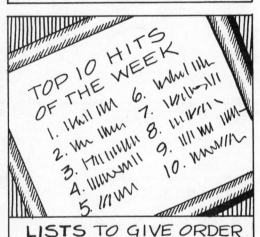

GREAT! HOW CAN I REMEMBER ALL THIS?

HERE ARE THE OTHER **5** MENTAL PROGRAMMES.

PICTURES

IMAGINATION

COLOUR

RHYTHM

SPACE

ONE **PICTURE** IS WORTH 1,000 WORDS.

WE USE **IMAGINATION** TO CREATE.

COLOUR ATTRACTS ATTENTION AND HELPS MEMORY.

RHYTHM HELPS MAKE THE RIGHT MATCH.

4FT

THE RIGHT **SPACE** MAKES US FEEL COMFORTABLE WITH OTHERS.

16

EXERCISE 2
Trigger Fingers

Trigger fingers form the foundation of this programme. You need to have these at your finger tips before proceeding!

The following exercise will help you with your trigger fingers.

Read the following story:

You buy a lottery ticket and your *numbers* win! Lost for *words*, you know the *logic* of the situation calls for you to put the money in the bank. But when you think about your wish *lists*, there, amongst the *details*, are mental *pictures* you stored in your *imagination* all in full, glorious *colours*. There's your trip round the world on Concorde. You can hear the *rhythm* of the jets taking you into *space*.

Read the story again, this time placing the italic words on each of your respective trigger fingers. Start with the little finger on your left hand, as shown in the following diagram. As you read the trigger word, say it out loud as you tap your respective finger.

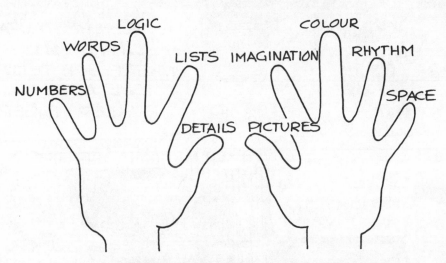

Read the story yet again and make certain you have each trigger finger placed correctly and remembered. Next repeat the story by referring to your trigger fingers only. This will take a few practises and, once you can do it, you will have placed all ten mental skills into your long-term memory.

3

The 3As

OUR STORY SO FAR . .
DISCOVERS HIS SUPERSELLF IN THE
MAGIC . HE GIVES FOR HER .
SUPERSELLF TEACHES ABOUT THE 10 MENTAL
SKILL PROGRAMMES and HOW TO REMEMBER
THEM ON HIS 10 TRIGGER FINGERS .
3 WEEKS LATER
BOB and SUE
GO TO THEIR FAVOURITE
CHINESE RESTAURANT
LANG CHU
WHERE BOB TELLS
SUE ABOUT
TRIGGER FINGERS.
SUE, THERE'S SOMETHING I'D LIKE TO TELL YOU!

BOB TELLS SUE ABOUT TRIGGER FINGERS.

HE SMILES AS HE TELLS HER THAT SALES HAVE SOARED 10% ALREADY.

I'VE ALSO DISCOVERED THE 3As!

TRIGGER FINGERS TEACH YOU TO BECOME **AWARE** OF YOUR **10** MENTAL SKILLS, **ANALYSE** OTHERS' SUCCESSFUL SALES PRESENTATIONS AND **ADAPT** THEM TO YOUR OWN SALES TECHNIQUES.

The **3As**
AWARENESS
ANALYSIS
ADAPTATION

IT'S AMAZINGLY SIMPLE and IT'S ALL AT YOUR FINGER TIPS.

LET'S TAKE A LOOK AT LONG CHU'S MENU...

AWARENESS

19

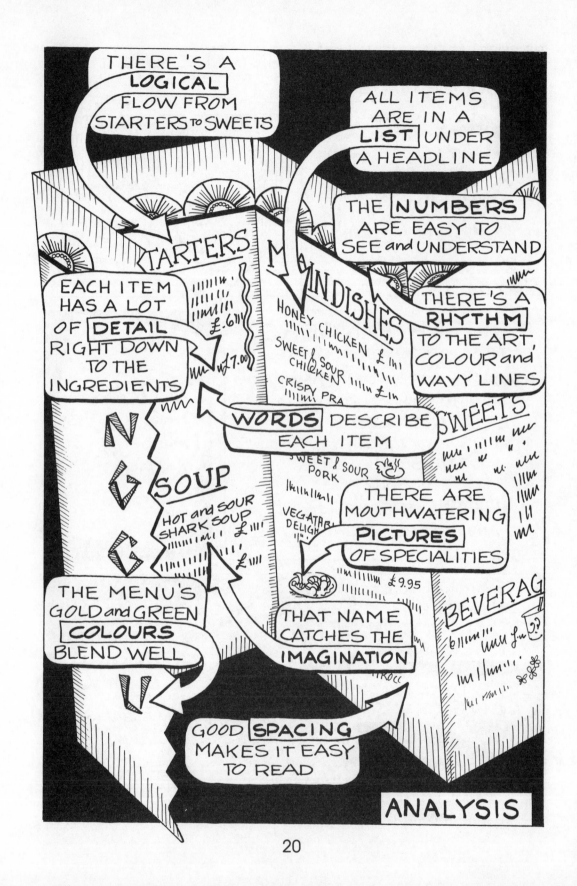

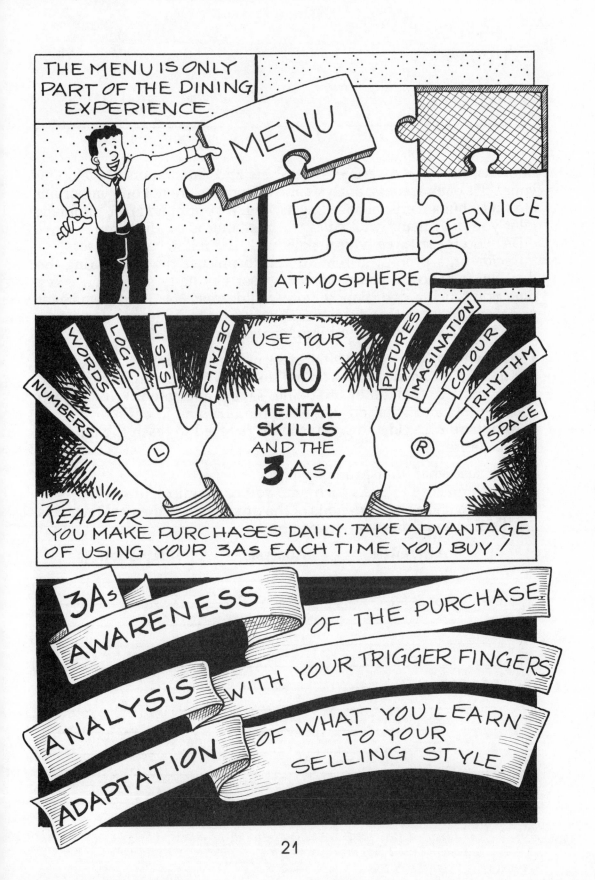

THE MENU IS ONLY PART OF THE DINING EXPERIENCE.

MENU

FOOD

SERVICE

ATMOSPHERE

USE YOUR 10 MENTAL SKILLS AND THE 3 As!

WORDS
LOGIC
LISTS
DETAILS
NUMBERS

PICTURES
IMAGINATION
COLOUR
RHYTHM
SPACE

READER
YOU MAKE PURCHASES DAILY. TAKE ADVANTAGE OF USING YOUR 3As EACH TIME YOU BUY!

3As

AWARENESS OF THE PURCHASE

ANALYSIS WITH YOUR TRIGGER FINGERS.

ADAPTATION OF WHAT YOU LEARN TO YOUR SELLING STYLE.

EXERCISE 3
The 3As

The 3As stand for Awareness, Analysis and Adaptation. Developing your skills of awareness, analysis and adaptation are not only important life skills, but are crucial in selling as well. If your mind is on automatic pilot you miss many vital clues the customer is sending you.

Develop these three critical skills with the following exercise.

Decide on a prompt to remind you to practise the 3As during the day. For instance, if you choose the door handle as a prompt, every time you touch a door handle you would apply the 3As to whatever you were doing at that moment. For example, whenever you open a door for a client, you would immediately apply the 3As:

- **Awareness.** Be aware of that exact moment in time.
- **Analysis.** Consider what you are doing, what you are saying, who you are with, what they are doing, saying and so on. Why are you doing this and what do you want the outcome to be?
- **Adaptation.** Decide how you should proceed to reach the outcome you desire.

Decide *now* what your prompt will be.

Start to practise the 3As each time you come into contact with your prompt. To make you conscious of the process, over the next few days list the first ten times you engage in it.

	Awareness	Analysis	Adaptation
1.			
2.			
3.			
4.			
5.			
6.			
7.			
8.			
9.			
10.			

4
Sales Senses

DRIVING HOME FROM **LONG CHU.**

THAT'S A GREAT RESTAURANT, SUE

The ATMOSPHERE, THE AROMAS, THE TASTES, THE SOUNDS ALL ADD UP TO THE WHOLE DINING EXPERIENCE.

THERE ARE **5** WAYS TO PLACE INFORMATION INTO YOUR CUSTOMER'S BRAIN.

SOUND

SIGHT

SMELL

TOUCH

TASTE

USE YOUR SALES SENSES!

SOUND

SIGHT

SMELL

TASTE

TOUCH

LONG CHU USED **5** SENSES

REMEMBER

HOW EYE CATCHING EVERYTHING WAS?

... AND HOW ABOUT ALL THOSE DIFFERENT TASTES?

THE SOUND OF THE SIZZLING OYSTERS, THE MUSIC, THE CRUNCHY NOODLES.?

EVEN THE CHOPSTICKS FELT DIFFERENT!

THE WONDERFUL AROMAS THAT FILLED THE AIR?

HOW GOOD THE WHOLE DINING EXPERIENCE FELT?

THESE ARE CALLED SALES SENSES and I STARTED USING THEM DAILY AT WORK.

REMEMBER IT IS

AWARENESS OF YOUR TRIGGER FINGERS WHEN MAKING A PURCHASE.

ANALYSIS USE YOUR TRIGGER FINGERS TO ANALYSE WHAT YOUR CUSTOMER WANTS.

ADAPTATION NEW ADAPT THIS INFORMATION TO INCREASE YOUR SALES.

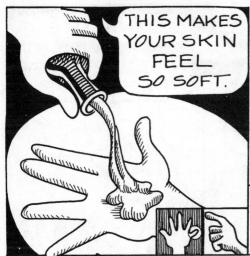

26

EXERCISE 4
Sales Senses

Now it's time to develop a new set of trigger fingers – your Sales Senses. We'll place the first five Sales Senses on your right hand. An easy way to do this is to touch all five senses with your five respective fingers. Start by placing your thumb on your ear, next your index finger on your eyes, your third finger on your nose, your fourth finger on your mouth and finally your little finger on your hand. The fingers represent the senses of hearing, seeing, smelling, tasting and touching respectively. Practise these a few times. Say each word as you touch the sense with the appropriate finger.

For the second part of this exercise, take one of the current products or services you are selling (if you are not currently selling, invent a product) and determine, as Sue did, how you could use each of your five senses to appeal to your customers' senses.

Product/service: _____

Sound _____

_____

Sight _____

_____

Smell _____

_____

Taste _____

_____

Touch _____

5
Selling's *Golden Rules*

DO YOU THINK HE'S TELLING THE TRUTH?

OH TIFFANY, I really love you!

LATER THAT EVENING

oh, yes.

DO YOU REALLY LOVE ME?

HE'S LYING!

BOB, CAN'T YOU SEE HE'S LYING?

HOW CAN YOU TELL?

HE'S SAYING ONE THING AND DOING ANOTHER.

LOOK AT HIS BODY LANGUAGE!

HIS EXPRESSION and TONE OF VOICE!

YOU'RE RIGHT, HE IS LYING!

THEY ARE DEAD GIVEAWAYS!

SOMETIMES MY CUSTOMERS ACT LIKE THEY DON'T BELIEVE ME.

BOB, DO YOU ALWAYS TELL THE TRUTH?

WELL, AH, MOST OF THE TIME.

MOST OF THE TIME?

DO YOU WANT A SALESPERSON TO LIE TO YOU WHEN YOU ARE THE CUSTOMER? JUST THINK HOW IT FEELS TO BE LIED TO!!

THE SALES PROFESSION RECEIVES A BAD MARK EVERY TIME A SALESPERSON DOESN'T TELL THE **TRUTH!!**

YOU'RE RIGHT, SUE.

BOB, DO YOU LOVE ME?

I DO, SUE, AND YOU KNOW THAT'S THE TRUTH!

SELLING'S GOLDEN RULES

- BE TRUTHFUL

- TREAT YOUR CUSTOMER AS YOU WOULD LIKE TO BE TREATED

EXERCISE 5
Selling's Golden Rules

Chances are that, no matter what you are selling, you spend a part of each day being a customer! How do salespeople treat you when you are the customer? In the following exercise list, in column 1, the last ten items you can remember buying from a salesperson, cashier or waiter. Then think back to each purchase and rate the quality of each buying experience – the way the salesperson, cashier or waiter treated you. On the following scale, 10 is excellent and 0 dreadful.

Buying experience	Quality of buying experience
1. _____	10 9 8 7 6 5 4 3 2 1 0
2. _____	10 9 8 7 6 5 4 3 2 1 0
3. _____	10 9 8 7 6 5 4 3 2 1 0
4. _____	10 9 8 7 6 5 4 3 2 1 0
5. _____	10 9 8 7 6 5 4 3 2 1 0
6. _____	10 9 8 7 6 5 4 3 2 1 0
7. _____	10 9 8 7 6 5 4 3 2 1 0
8. _____	10 9 8 7 6 5 4 3 2 1 0
9. _____	10 9 8 7 6 5 4 3 2 1 0
10. _____	10 9 8 7 6 5 4 3 2 1 0

What conclusions can you draw from your experiences? This exercise is a good example of the 3As. First, you became aware of the buying experience, next you analyse it and, finally, you decide how to adapt the lesson to your own selling style.

31

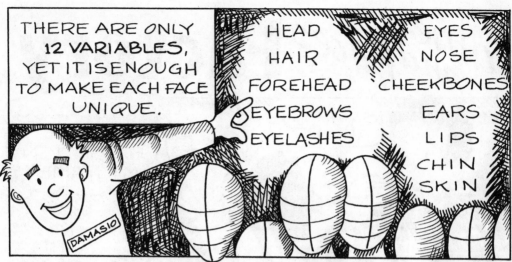

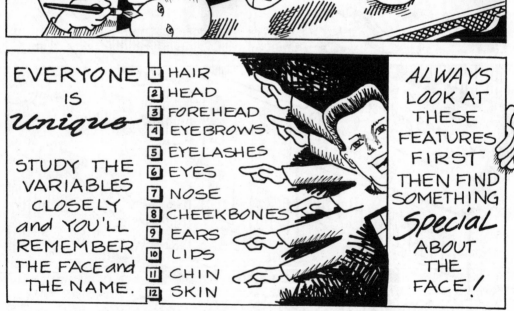

32

ONE WAY TO REMEMBER IS TO LOOK FOR SOMETHING *Special*

USE IMAGINATION, ASSOCIATION and LOCATION TO REMEMBER NAMES and FACES

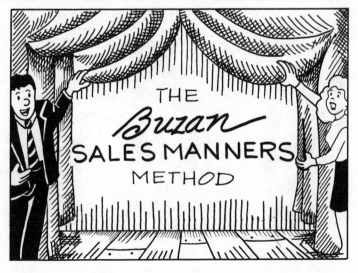

AND HERE'S ANOTHER WAY TO REMEMBER NAMES and FACES!

34

EXERCISE 6
Names and Faces

You use association, pre-existing knowledge, and your imagination to remember names and faces. The following exercise is based on names and faces you already know and will help you remember future customers' names and faces.

On the left list the names of ten of your favourite customers. Then, on the right, use your imagination to select some of their characteristics to help you remember their names.

Of course, you already know their names; however, this exercise is meant to show you how to apply the 3As technique to learning names and faces. It shows you how to become aware of customers' names and faces, analyse their features and adapt this knowledge (by using your imagination and associations) to store it in your long-term memory. Once you've seen how the 3As technique works, you'll be able to do it mentally as you encounter new customers.

Name	Characteristics
1. _____	_____
2. _____	_____
3. _____	_____
4. _____	_____
5. _____	_____
6. _____	_____
7. _____	_____
8. _____	_____
9. _____	_____
10. _____	_____

7
Infowealth

6 WEEKS LATER

BOB'S SALES ARE STILL CLIMBING *at* ACE PROPERTIES!

HI, BOB! HERE'S A LETTER FROM UNCLE MARK.

I WISH WE WERE RICH LIKE HIM.

HOW DID HE GET HIS MONEY?

HE HAS A SECRET FORMULA!

and I've learned that customers pay handsomely for the *RIGHT* INFORMATION!!!

SUPERSELLF, DO YOU KNOW THE SECRET FORMULA?

LATER THAT NIGHT

37

BE AN EXPERT

EDUCATE YOUR CUSTOMERS *Continually* IN THIS SEQUENCE:

1. DECIDE ON AN AREA of EXPERTISE
2. COLLECT DATA
3. STUDY
4. PRACTISE
5. DELIVER

HERE IT IS, BOB!

1. DECIDE ON AN AREA of EXPERTISE.

BE SPECIFIC FINANCING INDUSTRIAL PROPERTIES

WHEN YOU GIVE YOUR BRAIN A GOAL OR DIRECTION IT GOES ON A *SEARCH and FIND* MISSION LIKE A GUIDED MISSLE.

2. COLLECT DATA.

3. STUDY.

WITH FRIENDS. INTO A TAPE. TALK TO YOURSELF IN A MIRROR.

4. PRACTISE.

WRITE NEWSLETTERS. SPEAK AT MEETINGS. TO CUSTOMERS.

5. DELIVER.

EXERCISE 7
Infowealth

To help you become part of the information economy and enjoy info-wealth here, in an expanded format, are the 4 steps that SuperSellf presented to Bob.

Complete the following in as much detail as you can. Refer back to it, update it, act on it and you are on your way to infowealth.

1. Area of Expertise

_____

2. Collect data from
Presentations: _____
Libraries: _____
Colleges: _____
Associations: _____
Newsletters: _____
Experts: _____
Trade publications: _____
Trade offices: _____
The Internet: _____
Competitors: _____
Seminars: _____
Other: _____

3. Study
Best day/s: _____
Best times: _____
Duration of study: _____
Best place: _____
Resources needed: _____
Deadlines to meet: _____
Other: _____

4. Practise
Writing: _____
Speaking: _____
Feedback: _____
Other: _____

5. Deliver

Writing: _____

Publishing: _____

Newsletters: _____

Speaking: _____

Other: _____

Mind Mapping®

LANA TAKES A BREAK FROM HER SCHOOLWORK TO VISIT HER AUNTIE SUE.

HOW'S SCHOOL, LANA?

SO HAS YOUR UNCLE.

WE HAVE SO MUCH TO DO THIS TERM!

BOB IS STUDYING TO BECOME AN EXPERT IN FINANCING INDUSTRIAL WAREHOUSES.

LANA and BOB, I CAN SHOW YOU AN EASY WAY TO ORGANIZE ALL THIS NEW INFORMATION.

... AND RECALL IT AT WILL.

TURN A PLAIN PIECE of PAPER HORIZONTALLY and DRAW A PICTURE OF YOUR TOPIC IN THE CENTRE.

DO YOU HAVE SOME COLOURED PENS?

NEXT ADD MAIN BRANCHES LIKE A TREE and PRINT THE MAIN TOPICS OF INTEREST.

MAKE CERTAIN YOU ONLY USE ONE WORD PER LINE.

THIS IS LOOKING LIKE A MAP.

KEEP ADDING DETAILS to the BRANCHES.

A MIND MAP WORKS JUST LIKE THE BRAIN BY LINKING ALL THE BRANCHES TO THE CENTRAL IMAGE.

IT'S IMPORTANT TO USE **KEY WORDS** ON THOSE BRANCHES.

KEY

WHAT'S A KEY WORD?

A **KEY WORD** IS ANY WORD THAT HELPS YOU UNDERSTAND and RECALL THE ESSENCE OF A MAIN IDEA OR CONCEPT. KEY WORDS ARE USUALLY NOUNS – PEOPLE, PLACES and THINGS – AS WELL AS VERBS – *ACTION* WORDS. WHEN SELECTING KEY WORDS FOR YOUR MIND MAPS ASK YOURSELF IF THAT WORD IS NEEDED TO HELP YOU UNDERSTAND THE TOPIC THAT YOU ARE DEALING WITH.

HERE BOB – READ THE FOLLOWING PASSAGE AND UNDERLINE THE KEY WORDS.

(Suggested answers appear at the bottom of the page.)

Albert Einstein is known to many as one of the greatest brains of all time. What was the key to his incredible success? Well, a great many of his achievements were the result of his vivid imagination. One sunny day, for example, Einstein was sitting on top of a large, green hill and he started daydreaming. He imagined that he was riding through the universe on a sunbeam. However, he was really confused when, at the end of his rather odd journey, he returned right back to where his trip had begun. After thinking about the possible meaning of this daydream, Einstein arrived at the notion that the universe must be curved. A result of this imaginative adventure was Albert Einstein's formulation of the Theory of Relativity.

Suggested answers: Albert Einstein, brains, key, success, imagination, daydreaming, riding sunbeam, returned, begun, universe, curved, Theory of Relativity.

45

RESEARCH SHOWS THAT THE BRAIN REMEMBERS MORE WHEN YOU BREAK UP YOUR STUDY PERIODS RATHER THAN *PUSHING* YOURSELF TO EXHAUSTION and SUFFERING **STRESS**.

IT'S IMPORTANT TO TAKE A **5-10** MINUTE BREAK *EVERY* 50 MINUTES

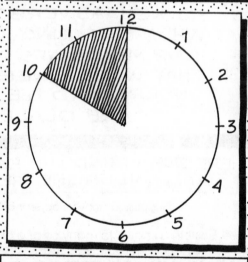

TAKE REGULAR BREAKS WHEN STUDYING.

DO OTHER THINGS IN YOUR BREAK

- ☐ WALK
- ☐ PHONE A FRIEND
- ☐ DANCE TO YOUR FAVOURITE TUNE
- ☐ EXERCISE
- ☐ PLAY A MUSICAL INSTRUMENT
- ☐ MAKE UP YOUR OWN ACTIVITY

TIP MAKE SURE YOU DO SOMETHING TOTALLY DIFFERENT IN YOUR BREAKS

46

HERE ARE SOME SYMBOLS MADE WITH **CIRCLES**

COPY THESE
SYMBOLS
OR USE
TRACING
PAPER
TO PRACTISE

AND SOME MADE WITH **TRIANGLES**

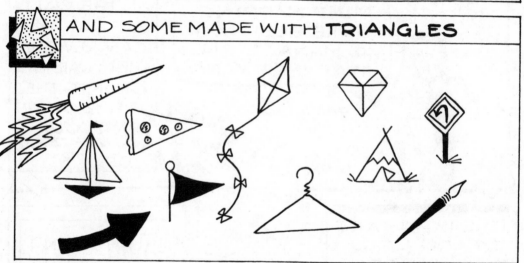

AND **RECTANGLES** AND **SQUARES**

ONE WAY

MEMO

AND **COMBINATIONS,**

AND **OVALS**

AND WITH **LINES.**

HERE ARE SOME IN **3D**

AND **FACES**

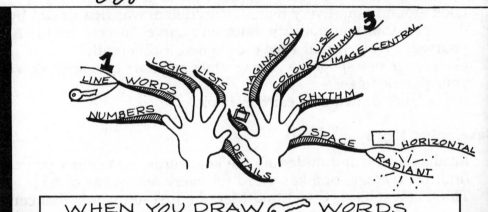

WHEN YOU DRAW 🔑 WORDS
AND SYMBOLS ∞♡! THEY ACT AS.....
MIND TRIGGERS.

- STUDY SMART WITH MIND MAPS
- COPY
- TAKE BREAKS
- REVIEW

MIND MAPPING
HELPS YOU TO BECOME
AN EXPERT
AT SCHOOL and WORK
BY HELPING YOU TO REMEMBER
MORE and ≡FASTER.
PRACTISE
MIND MAPPING
EVERY DAY and INFOWEALTH
IS ON ITS WAY.

EXERCISE 8
Mind Mapping®

To help develop your Mind Mapping you need to play with your drawing skills and practise selecting key words. Continue to construct Maps whenever possible.

Developing Drawing Skills

1. Draw daily, even if it's only for a few minutes. Carry some paper with you so that you can sketch at odd moments. Draw anything that comes to mind when you have a free moment.
2. Look around you. Every manufactured item was first drawn by a designer. Can you trace the lines and curves in your mind? Ask yourself: "How would I have designed it differently?"
3. Go through newspapers and magazines and trace over artwork with your pen or finger.
4. Buy a basic drawing or cartoon book.

Developing Key Word Skills

1. Read an article and underline the key words. Remember you can find, on average, one key word for every ten words of text.
2. Think of a subject, then Mind Map the first ten words that come to mind. From these ten key words write a 100-word article.
3. Read through a product brochure and mark the key words. See how much easier it is to remember.

Developing Mind Mapping Skills

Tie together your new drawing skills with your key word skills as you create your Mind Map. Keep your Mind Maps on a separate pad so that you can review your progress. Here are some subjects that you can Mind Map daily.

1. The daily newspaper.
2. Customers you contacted today.
3. The products and services you sold today.
4. Competitors' products and services you heard about today.
5. Your daily diary, sales appointments, sales meetings, sales articles and so on.
6. The morning and/or lunchtime and/or evening news on radio or television.

7. Books you're reading.
8. Your 'To do' list.
9. Your weekend.
10. Your holiday.

To be an expert in Mind Mapping you need to complete about 100 Mind Maps. If you Mind Map five of the above daily you would be an expert Mind Mapper in less than a month!

9
The *Right* Packaging

9

AS BOB'S **30**TH BIRTHDAY APPROACHES SUE MENTALLY PLANS HIS PARTY

HAPPY BIRTHDAY, BOB SURPRISE!

SUE INVITES THE GUESTS

BOB CERTAINLY IS BECOMING A *SUPERSELLF!*

ANY PRESENT TO HELP IMPROVE HIS MIND OR HIS BODY!

THE BIRTHDAY ARRIVES

LOOK AT ALL THESE GIFTS!

The Right Packaging

Here are some additional exercises to develop the six components that make up the 'right packaging' mentioned at Bob's birthday party.

Voice

Take any book or article and read aloud from it for three to four minutes every day. This simple exercise will make a dramatic difference to your sales voice in terms of projection, pitch, flow and rhythm. You will notice the difference in days! If you have a tape recorder, record yourself and study the recordings.

Clothing

How would you rate your eye for colour coordination and knowing the right clothes to wear for the appropriate occasions? This is an area on which there is a great deal of published information. Spend some time researching the subject of clothing. If you can afford it, have a clothing consultant advise you. Mind Map your new look.

Physical Health

Have you had a medical check-up during the last 18 months? If not, why not? Your health is your greatest asset! Do you have an exercise programme that you do regularly, three to four times a week? This can be as simple as walking for twenty minutes.

Are you eating a balanced diet? Do you need to lose some weight? Answering these questions will lead you to become aware of your health, analyse it and adapt to the changes needed to make your life both healthier and happier. Mind Map the new healthier you.

Appearance

Become aware of your demeanour. How do you walk, sit, run, hold your body, gesticulate? Analyse these important movements by observing yourself in a mirror or have a friend video you. Learn about poise and then adapt your new knowledge to improve your appearance.

Mental Alertness

Do the daily crossword in the newspaper. Buy a book of puzzles and work through it. Regularly play games such as chess, Go, Monopoly and card games such as bridge. If you have a musical instrument, play it. If not, buy a simple recorder or flute. Sing along to your favourite songs. Develop hobbies and outside interests, attend lectures and read books on a wide range of subjects. Keep Mind Maps of your new learning.

Stress Management

You can reduce your stress level with simple breathing exercises, such as the following. Keeping your eyes closed throughout, take a deep breath, pushing down your diaphragm so that the air goes deep into your lungs. Continue to inhale, expanding the chest. Then exhale deeply, relaxing your shoulders and chest and contracting your diaphragm to expel all the air from your lungs. Silently say 'Ten-relax'. Repeat the process for the second breath, saying 'Nine-relax'. Count down to one.

10
The COMPLETE Picture

ROBERT! THESE SPECS ARE ALL MESSED UP!

BACK AT WORK BOB HAS A PROBLEM.

LATER THAT NIGHT

I'VE COME A LONG WAY BUT I'M STILL MAKING SILLY MISTAKES!

I CAN TELL YOU WHY and HOW TO GET THE DETAILS RIGHT.

FIRST

LEARN TO FOCUS ON WHAT YOU ARE DOING.

WHAT DO YOU MEAN, *SUPERSELLF?*

THINK OF YOUR ATTENTION AS A *TORCH BEAM.*

WHERE YOU SHINE IT IS WHERE YOUR FOCUS IS.

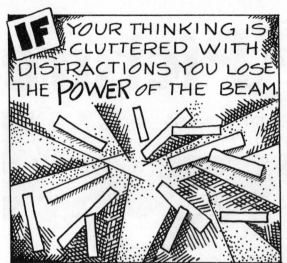

IF YOUR THINKING IS CLUTTERED WITH DISTRACTIONS YOU LOSE THE **POWER** OF THE BEAM.

The Secret is TO BE INTERESTED IN WHAT YOU ARE DOING. THAT WAY YOU FOCUS 100% OF YOUR ATTENTION LIKE A LASER BEAM.

SECOND WE STORE INFORMATION IN PICTURES.

TRY THIS - DESCRIBE YOUR FRONT DOOR.

IT'S MADE OF WOOD, WITH A GLASS PANEL and a SPY HOLE.

GOOD, DID YOU NOTICE YOU WERE DESCRIBING A PICTURE?

WHAT IS YOUR FAVOURITE DESSERT?

ICE CREAM!

IS THAT WITH CHOCOLATE PIECES?

OH, NO!

WITH NUTS and A CHERRY?

NO, WITH HOT FUDGE.

IF YOU DON'T SAY ALL THE DETAILS, THE LISTENER'S BRAIN WILL FILL IN ITS OWN DETAILS.

IT IS THE SAME WITH **SELLING**. YOU MUST HAVE <u>ALL</u> THE DETAILS FROM YOUR CUSTOMER OR YOUR BRAIN WILL MAKE THEM UP.

AND YOU MAY DRAW THE WRONG CONCLUSIONS.

AH YES, I AM GETTING THE PICTURE.

NEXT TIME

YOU ARE GETTING INFORMATION FROM A CUSTOMER — BE INTERESTED, FOCUSED and THINK IN PICTURES.

61

EXERCISE 10

The Complete Picture Method

In recent years visual dictionaries have become available. Make sure you have one – they are excellent tools for helping you develop the complete picture method.

Below is a series of words for you to turn into mental pictures. Note that if the description is not detailed enough you tend to fill it in with your own details. That's why it's so important to get all those details from your customer. You want to make sure you are selling your customer what *they* really want, not what you think they want! The descriptions below vary in their amount of detail and seriousness. This will help you develop your complete picture skills.

1. A gold ring.
2. An 18-inch external satellite dish.
3. A set of tools comprising a hammer, small screwdriver, spanner, pliers and knife.
4. A medium-sized pizza, steaming hot and loaded with assorted toppings.
5. A roaring lion.
6. Rod Stewart in concert.
7. A tin of baked beans.
8. An open, empty deckchair on a deserted cold and windy beach.
9. A football travelling in mid-air.
10. Two slices of bread and butter on a plate.
11. A tie.
12. A pair of red leather boxing gloves signed by Muhammed Ali.
13. A portable laptop computer with a colour monitor.
14. An overweight, friendly, brown and white corgi dog (without a tail).
15. A medieval castle.
16. A violin.
17. A hand-held mini-television.
18. A helicopter in mid-air.
19. A CD of your favourite artist.
20. A bunch of black grapes.

Power Hooks

UPDATE

WEEK
18
SUPERSELLF
DEVELOPMENT
PROGRAMME

£

* NOT EVERY WEEK IS AN UP WEEK FOR BOB, BUT HE LEARNS FROM HIS MISTAKES AND HIS PROGRESS CONTINUES.

LOOK AT HIS SALES PROGRESS

WEEKS

5 WEEKS *after* HIS BIRTHDAY.

BOB HAS IMPROVED HIS APPEARANCE and ENERGY BY WORKING ON HIS MIND and BODY.

I WONDER IF MY CUSTOMERS REMEMBER ME?

QUIZ
COUNT THE NUMBER OF CHANGES IN BOB'S FEATURES SINCE HE MET *SuperSellf*

YES, THEY DO and HERE'S A NEW TECHNIQUE TO MAKE SURE THEY REMEMBER YOU *forever!*

YOUR CUSTOMER'S MEMORY IS LIKE A FILING CABINET.

CLEANERS

THE CUSTOMER DECIDES WHAT TO REMEMBER and PLACES IT ON A **MEMORY HOOK**

IT GETS TURNED INTO A PICTURE

WHICH IS STORED IN **LONG-TERM MEMORY.**

IN MEMORY

RECALL OUT

HAIRCUT AT 2 PM

WHEN THE CUSTOMER NEEDS THE INFORMATION IT ZOOMS OUT ON **RECALL HOOKS**

ONCE YOU KNOW THE **5** POWER HOOKS OF RECALL YOU'LL HAVE IT!

5 POWER HOOKS
- ✓ BEGINNING
- ✓ PERSONAL INVOLVEMENT
- ✓ OUTSTANDING
- ✓ REPEATED
- ✓ ENDING

WHY NOT TURN THEM *into* TRIGGER FINGERS *and* PLACE THEM *on* YOUR LEFT HAND.

PERSONAL INVOLVEMENT

BEGINNING

UNUSUAL OR OUTSTANDING

REPEATED

ENDING

SEE IT
SAY IT
TAP IT
USE IT

THE NEXT DAY BOB USES *POWER HOOKS* AT ACE.

I FOUND JUST WHAT YOU WANTED, MR YOUNG.

BEGINNING

ENDING

I'LL BRING THE CONTRACTS ROUND TOMORROW AND YOU CAN MOVE IN NEXT WEDNESDAY

HOLD THESE PLANS WHILE I EXPLAIN THE LAYOUT TO YOU.

PERSONAL INVOLVEMENT

REPEATED

ONCE AGAIN, YOU WON'T HAVE TO SPEND £1,000 TO BUILD REFRIGERATION

UNUSUAL

NOTICE IT HAS 6 REFRIGERATION ROOMS, SO THERE IS NO EXTRA *COST*

FOR YOUR NEXT MEMORABLE SALES CONVERSATION USE YOUR **5** *POWER HOOKS* AND THE CUSTOMER WILL REMEMBER YOU.

EXERCISE 11
Power Hooks

You have just discovered the five power hooks that help you enter and remain in your customer's mind! These hooks work equally well with both the written and spoken word. Make certain that these are at your finger tips by placing them on your left hand. Start with the little finger on your left hand as shown in the following diagram. As you read the trigger word, say it out loud as you tap your respective finger.

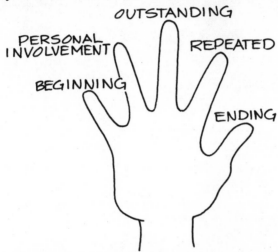

Imagine you are writing a sales letter to a customer regarding a new product or service.

Become aware of the five power hooks and decide how you could incorporate them into your letter. You can use the following layout or, even better, Mind Map the letter using the space on page 70.

1. Beginning

2. Personal involvement

3. Outstanding

4. Repeated

5. Ending

Mind Map your letter in the space below.

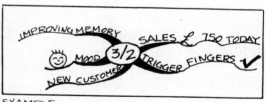

EXAMPLE

12

Inner Modelling®

SUE IS WORRIED ABOUT HER SALES PRESENTATION AT A WOMEN'S CLUB NEXT WEEK

SUNDAY, BOB and SUE GO ON A PICNIC.

YOUR PRESENTATION WILL BE GREAT! YOU ARE AN EXPERT.

I AM SO NERVOUS!

TRUE, BUT THE LAST TIME I GAVE A SPEECH MY LEGS BEGAN TO SHAKE

SIGH

I FEEL NERVOUS WHEN I'M ABOUT TO MEET AN IMPORTANT CLIENT AS WELL.

YOU SOUND AS IF YOU NEED SOME *SuperSelf* HELP!

MAKE IT DETAILED and RUN IT THROUGH YOUR MIND SEVERAL TIMES *Slowly* AT FIRST THEN ≡SPEED IT UP! ADD COLOUR and GOOD FEELINGS

THAT WAS GREAT! NOW I'M LOOKING FOWARD TO DOING MY PRESENTATION.

ONE WEEK LATER

AND THAT'S THE LATEST INFO ON LIPSTICK!

THANK YOU!

and THANK YOU, SUPERSELLF!

BRAVO!

ACTUALLY EVERY SALE HAPPENS TWICE.

FIRST

THEN

FIRST IN YOUR MIND

THEN IN REAL TIME

MENTALLY *PRACTISE* WHAT YOU ARE ABOUT TO EXPERIENCE BEFORE YOU DO IT.

YOU CAN MENTALLY PRACTISE COLD CALLING, WRITING SALES LETTERS, MAKING A SALES PRESENTATION.... Anything. JUST DO IT!

I HAVE AN IMPORTANT SALES MEETING TOMORROW.

IT'S LIKE MAKING UP A MENTAL MOVIE.

EXERCISE 12
Inner Modelling®

Inner modelling is so easy to do and is extremely effective. Yet, like anything else you learn, it requires practice. Think of how you use Inner Modelling in everyday life – for example, to plan your holidays or a special party. You keep running a movie of the future event in your mind, and in great detail, until it actually happens. Now you can use the same technique to improve your sales.

Select an item or service that you enjoy selling. Next, invent the ideal customer to buy it. With your eyes closed run a mental movie of the complete sales presentation, including your product/service and the customer. Re-run this movie adding a soundtrack of your sales conversation. Simply make it up! Put your 20 trigger fingers to work.

Re-run the movie, with the soundtrack, again. This time, add feelings – the good feelings you enjoyed while selling to your ideal customer, the feeling of accomplishment when you satisfy the customer, the glow of a job well done.

You can vary future mental rehearsals by changing the item or service you are selling, making the customer more resistant to buying and so on. Add anything you like.

Don't "practise" selling with the customer when you can get all the practice you need in your mind!

13

Brain Sell *Compass*

SUPERSELLF HAS SURPRISED BOB and SUE WITH *SPECIAL* GIFTS.

WOW! MATCHING COMPASS WATCHES.

I WONDER HOW THEY WORK?

HERE ARE THE INSTRUCTIONS

BRAIN ⊘ SELL COMPASS INSTRUCTIONS

THIS COMPASS WILL TELL YOU WHICH MENTAL SKILL YOUR CUSTOMER IS USING.

READER: WHY NOT CUT OUT THIS COMPASS AND USE IT FOR EASY REFERENCE.

THE NEXT DAY

THE CUSTOMER IS USING SIGHT.

LOOK IN THE MIRROR and SEE FOR YOURSELF.

SIGHT

I CAN IMAGINE HOW NICE THIS WILL LOOK WITH MY NEW DRESS.

YES, IMAGINE ALL THE COMPLIMENTS YOU WILL RECEIVE.

BOB TRIED HIS NEW COMPASS, too!

IS THERE ANYTHING ELSE I CAN DO FOR YOU, MR STEVENS?

YES, I'D LIKE TO SPEAK TO SOME OF YOUR CLIENTS.

I MUST MATCH WORDS AND SOUNDS.

SOUNDS

WORDS

WORDS and SOUNDS

HERE ARE SOME **NAMES** and **NUMBERS** YOU CAN CALL.

THANKS, BOB.

HEY, AFTER DOING THIS A FEW TIMES IT BECOMES AUTOMATIC.

LATER THAT WEEK

I MADE AN EXTRA SALE THIS WEEK USING MY BRAIN SELL COMPASS.

MY SALES WERE UP TOO, AND IT WAS SO EASY.

REMEMBER, IT BECOMES AUTOMATIC AFTER A FEW TIMES.

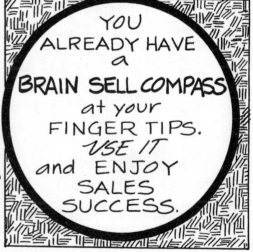

YOU ALREADY HAVE a **BRAIN SELL COMPASS** at your FINGER TIPS. *USE IT* and ENJOY SALES SUCCESS.

EXERCISE 13
Brain Sell Compass

Your Brain Sell compass comprises the 20 whole-brain skills you should now have at your finger tips (see page 89 for the trigger finger review). Photocopy this page and keep it with you or display it on your desk for quick and easy reference – that is, until using your trigger fingers becomes second nature.

A quick way to understand and apply your Brain Sell compass in sales is to use your experience as a customer. Each time you spend money, use a credit card or sign a cheque apply your Brain Sell compass or trigger fingers. This simple act of spending makes you aware of being the customer.

Next analyse, with your Brain Sell compass, which of the 20 whole-brain skills the salesperson is using on you and how effectively.

Finally, adapt. How can you apply what you have learnt as the customer to improve your sales performance?

Start using this approach immediately, today! List the next five items you buy and mentally review how well the Brain Sell compass was used.

1. _____
2. _____
3. _____
4. _____
5. _____

Once you have been on the receiving end of the Brain Sell compass you will be in a much stronger position to apply it to your customers.

14

The Big Picture

4 WEEKS LATER

LOOK WHAT'S HAPPENED, BOB, YOU'VE TURNED INTO A *Superself* and YOUR SALES AT ACE HAVE GONE THROUGH THE ROOF!!

CONGRATULATIONS TO BOTH OF YOU!

REMEMBER WHEN YOU BOUGHT THE MIRROR FOR SUE AND SAW ME FOR THE *FIRST* TIME?

HOW COULD I FORGET THE BEGINNING OF MY *SUPERSELLF* BRAIN SELL JOURNEY WITH YOU?

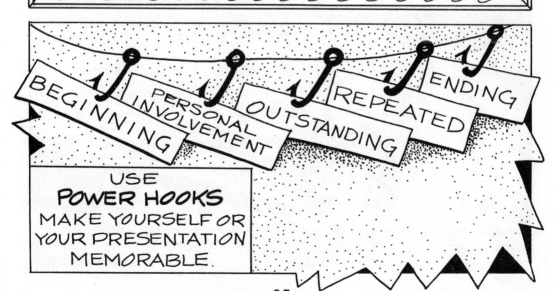

The Big Picture Quiz

"The Big Picture" reviews the total programme that transformed Bob and Sue into high-sales producers. Test your knowledge of the programme with the Big Picture Quiz. Answers are at the bottom of the page.

1. What are the two golden rules of selling? _____
    _____

2. The 3As stand for: _____

3. In the names and faces factory, a face comprised how many variables? _____

4. Name the ten trigger fingers on your left hand. _____
    _____

5. What are the five steps to the infowealth formula? _____
    _____

6. What are the six components that make up the right packaging?
    _____

7. Name the five power hooks. _____
    _____

8. Name the ten trigger fingers on your right hand. _____
    _____

9. All sales happen twice, first in your _____ then in _____ time. (Complete the blanks.)

10. The Brain Sell compass helps you _____ your customer's mental skills. (Complete the blank.)

88

Trigger Finger
REVIEW

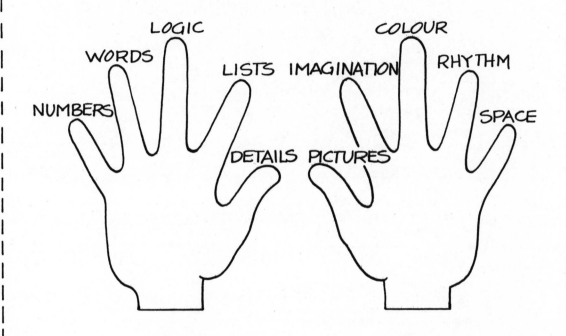

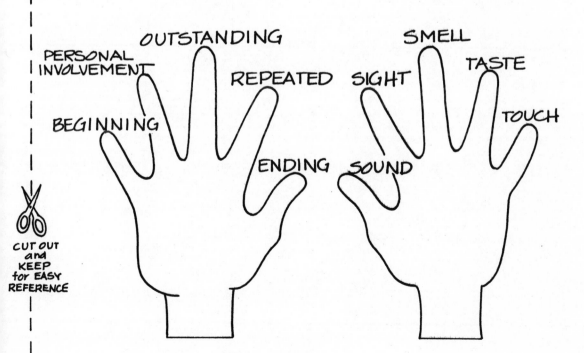

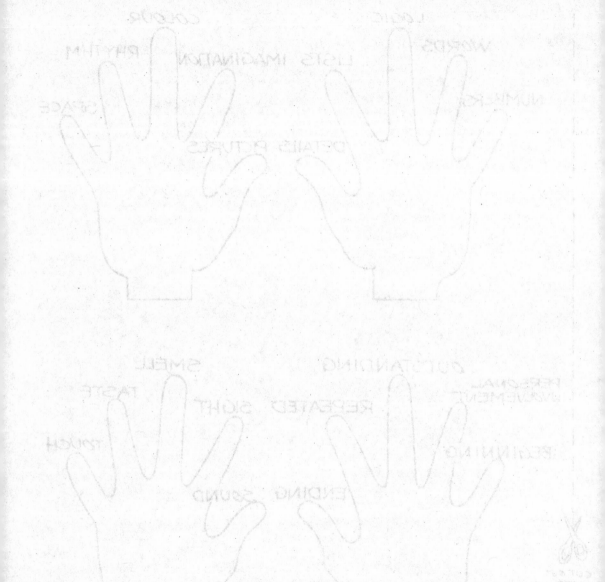

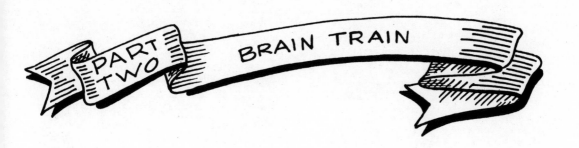

PART TWO

BRAIN TRAIN

The Brain Train WORKOUT

PROGRAMME

WITH YOUR PERSONAL TRAINER

DO YOU KNOW WHAT THE STRONGEST MUSCLE IS IN YOUR BODY ? THE ONE THAT NEEDS THE MOST OXYGEN and WORKING OUT?

SuperSellf

It's your brain! Yes, I know, that was a trick question, but the truth is a, pumped up, well exercised brain is the key to selling success. Like any muscle, the more you use your brain the stronger it becomes – and the better you can concentrate, make decisions, solve problems and sell creatively. Your IQ has nothing to do with it. Someone with a high IQ who has a lazy brain will accomplish less than a person with an "average" IQ who trains his or her brain.

So make yourself comfortable and prepare to start your brain train programme – no club to join, no equipment to buy – no sweat!

The Brain Train
W O R K O U T

The BRAIN TRAIN DIARY

1 THOUGHT MASTER

2 BRAIN BUDDIES

3 SENSE SATIONAL SELLING

4 TRIGGER FINGERS

5 SUPERIOR SALES MEMORY

6 BREATHING SPACE

7 SALES SPEAK

8 SALES DETECTIVE

INSTRUCTIONS

THIS PROGRAMME INVOLVES *DAILY* REPETITION OF 8 SIMPLE MENTAL SKILLBUILDERS CUSTOMIZED *for* IMPROVED SALES PERFORMANCE.

DO THEM FOR **30** DAYS AND WATCH YOUR SALES SOAR!

HERE'S HOW TO DO EACH ONE.

1 THOUGHT MASTER — FINAL NUMBER

The purpose of this exercise is to develop your powers of concentration while making you aware of intruding thoughts.

Concentrate on the second hand of a watch for one minute. While concentrating exclusively on that second hand, silently repeat the word "one". Should any distracting thought enter your mind (such as "Hungry, What's to eat?") move to the number "two" while maintaining your concentration. Should another thought intrude, move on to number "three" and so on until the minute is up. You might end up repeating the number "twenty" during those 60 seconds. This would mean that you experienced 20 intruding thoughts.

Record your score of intrusive thoughts in your diary. With daily practice you will increase your powers of concentration and reduce the number of intrusive thoughts.

You can increase the level of difficulty by watching the second hand without counting, or while humming your favourite tune or in a noisy room, with the TV or radio on!

2 BRAIN BUDDIES

Your brain is made up of a left and right cortex. Think of these as two buddies working together for the common goal of improving your sales.

The following workout strengthens the buddy that may have been lacking exercise in the past!

Each day copy the two lines on your diary page with your non-dominant hand (the one you don't normally write with). Record the time it takes for each line in the corresponding box.

Practising using all five senses to develop whole-brain pictures is fun. Take the word "OCEAN", for example.

In your mind, walk on a beach and feel the warm sand between your toes. Feel the salty ocean breeze sweep across your face. Hear the crashing waves and feel the salty spray on your skin. Smell the ocean breeze as you taste the salty spray hitting your lips.

Each day your diary will give you a new word so that you can create a whole-brain picture using your five senses.

You should have all 20 trigger fingers at your finger tips!

Each time you spend money, write a cheque or use a credit card you are a customer making a purchase. It's another opportunity to learn from your trigger fingers.

Being **aware** of the purchase triggers your fingers to **analyse** the sale and **adapt** your findings to improve your sales techniques.

Space is provided in the diary to list your daily purchases as a reminder to apply your trigger fingers analysis.

5 SUPERIOR SALES MEMORY

Each day your diary presents you with new memory-building exercises. These are all designed to improve your sales memory muscles.

6 BREATHING SPACE

Your brain needs periods of rest or you will suffer from brain burn-out! With discipline and concentration you will develop your BSB (Breathing Space Brain). You can use BSB any time you feel tired or stressed or when you need an added boost before making that important sales presentation!

The exercise requires you to sit or lie on your back, relax your body and close your eyes. Begin breathing easily, and simply listen to its sound. Should your attention drift away from your breath, gently bring it back. Continue for several minutes.

Then repeat the above exercise but this time, instead of concentrating on your breath, choose a word that has pleasant associations for you, such as calm, peace or wealth. Repeat that word silently to yourself each time you exhale. Continue for several minutes.

Words are the working tools of your sales brain. You need to build a strong sales vocabulary to improve your ability to communicate and understand your customers.

Each day find a new word to add to your sales vocabulary. Write the word and its definition in your diary and start to use it immediately.

Your sales brain is like a detective. When it recognizes and unravels the clues, you make the sale! Developing the sales detective part of your brain requires a daily riddle to be solved.

Take, for example, the riddle 16 = O in a P.
The answer is 16 ounces in a pound.

Suggested answers to the sales detective riddles can be found on page 130.

How to Complete Your Daily Diary

ENTER THE DAY •

THE DATE •

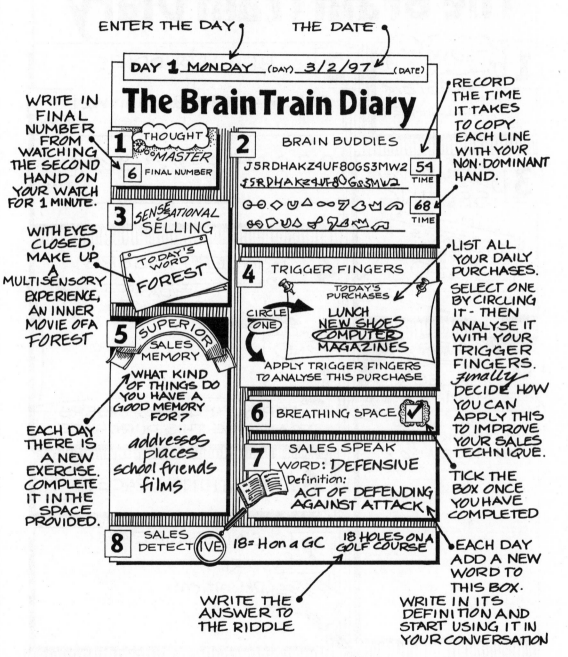

DAY **1** MONDAY (DAY) 3/2/97 (DATE)

The Brain Train Diary

WRITE IN FINAL NUMBER FROM WATCHING THE SECOND HAND ON YOUR WATCH FOR 1 MINUTE.

1 THOUGHT ZooMASTER
6 FINAL NUMBER

RECORD THE TIME IT TAKES TO COPY EACH LINE WITH YOUR NON·DOMINANT HAND.

2 BRAIN BUDDIES

JSRDHAKZ4UF8OGS3MW2 **54** TIME
JSRDHAKZ4UF8OGs3MW2

○Ɵ◇♡△∞Ɣ℈ɱ∽ **68** TIME
∽Ɵᴅ♡Ꮜ♂Ɣ∂ɱ∽

3 SENSESATIONAL SELLING

WITH EYES CLOSED, MAKE UP A MULTISENSORY EXPERIENCE, AN INNER MOVIE OF A FOREST

TODAY'S WORD FOREST

LIST ALL YOUR DAILY PURCHASES. SELECT ONE BY CIRCLING IT - THEN ANALYSE IT WITH YOUR TRIGGER FINGERS. *finally* DECIDE HOW YOU CAN APPLY THIS TO IMPROVE YOUR SALES TECHNIQUE.

4 TRIGGER FINGERS

TODAY'S PURCHASES

CIRCLE ONE

LUNCH
NEW SHOES
(COMPUTER)
MAGAZINES

APPLY TRIGGER FINGERS TO ANALYSE THIS PURCHASE

5 SUPERIOR SALES MEMORY

WHAT KIND OF THINGS DO YOU HAVE A GOOD MEMORY FOR?

addresses
places
school friends
films

EACH DAY THERE IS A NEW EXERCISE. COMPLETE IT IN THE SPACE PROVIDED.

6 BREATHING SPACE ✓

TICK THE BOX ONCE YOU HAVE COMPLETED

7 SALES SPEAK
WORD: DEFENSIVE
Definition:
ACT OF DEFENDING AGAINST ATTACK

8 SALES DETECT(IVE) 18= H on a GC 18 HOLES ON A GOLF COURSE

WRITE THE ANSWER TO THE RIDDLE

EACH DAY ADD A NEW WORD TO THIS BOX. WRITE IN ITS DEFINITION AND START USING IT IN YOUR CONVERSATION

The Brain Train Diary

1 THOUGHT MASTER

☐ FINAL NUMBER

2 BRAIN BUDDIES

JSRDHAKZ4UF80GS3MW2 _____

TIME

⚭◇♡△∞7ᗱ♡⌒ _____

TIME

3 SENSESATIONAL SELLING

TODAY'S WORD
BIRD

4 TRIGGER FINGERS

TODAY'S PURCHASES

CIRCLE ONE

APPLY TRIGGER FINGERS TO ANALYSE THIS PURCHASE

5 SUPERIOR SALES MEMORY

WHAT WERE YOU THINKING OF AN HOUR AGO?

6 BREATHING SPACE

7 SALES SPEAK

WORD:
Definition:

8 SALES DETECT IVE   7 = W of the W

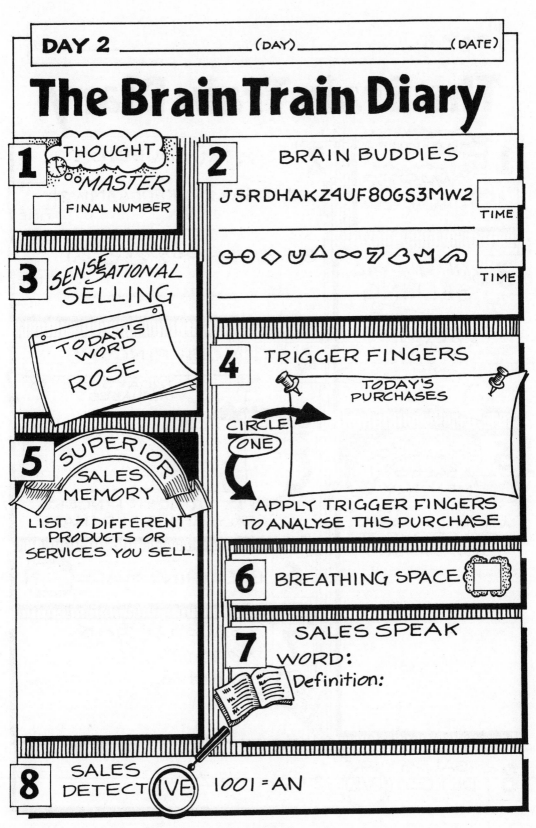

The Brain Train Diary

1 THOUGHT MASTER

☐ FINAL NUMBER

2 BRAIN BUDDIES

J5RDHAKZ4UF80GS3MW2

TIME

⌒⌒ ◇ ∪△ ∞ 7 ⌐ ↻ ⌒ ↻

TIME

3 SENSE SATIONAL SELLING

TODAY'S WORD

LEMON

4 TRIGGER FINGERS

TODAY'S PURCHASES

CIRCLE ONE

APPLY TRIGGER FINGERS TO ANALYSE THIS PURCHASE

5 SUPERIOR SALES MEMORY

WHAT DID YOU HAVE FOR BREAKFAST LAST SUNDAY?

6 BREATHING SPACE

7 SALES SPEAK

WORD:

Definition:

8 SALES DETECTIVE   12 = S of the Z

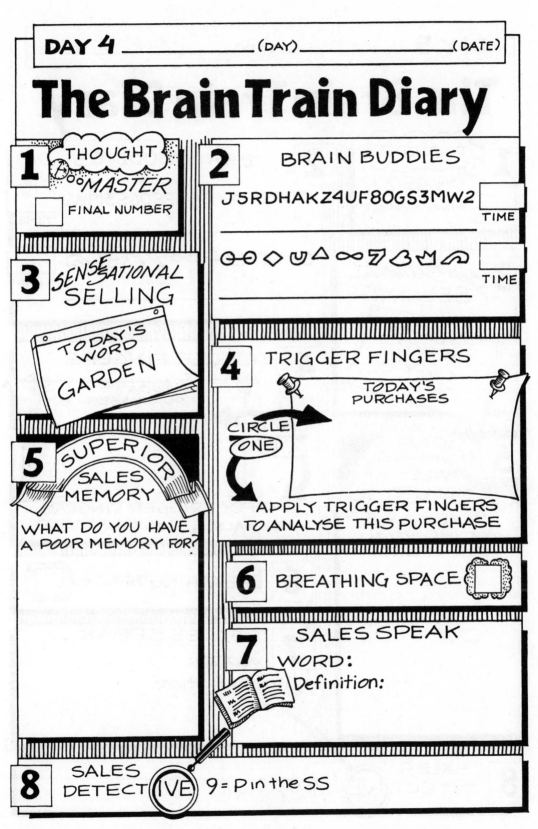

DAY 4 _____ (DAY) _____ (DATE)

The Brain Train Diary

1 THOUGHT MASTER
☐ FINAL NUMBER

2 BRAIN BUDDIES

J5RDHAKZ4UF80GS3MW2 [ ] TIME

⟨symbols⟩ [ ] TIME

3 SENSE SATIONAL SELLING

TODAY'S WORD
GARDEN

4 TRIGGER FINGERS
TODAY'S PURCHASES
CIRCLE ONE
APPLY TRIGGER FINGERS TO ANALYSE THIS PURCHASE

5 SUPERIOR SALES MEMORY
WHAT DO YOU HAVE A POOR MEMORY FOR?

6 BREATHING SPACE

7 SALES SPEAK
WORD:
Definition:

8 SALES DETECTIVE   9 = Pin the SS

The Brain Train Diary

1 THOUGHT MASTER

[ ] FINAL NUMBER

2 BRAIN BUDDIES

J5RDHAKZ4UF80GS3MW2

_____

TIME

⊙—⊙ ◇ ♡ △ ∞ 7 𝕵 ♡ ∽

_____

TIME

3 SENSE SATIONAL SELLING

TODAY'S WORD

SKY

4 TRIGGER FINGERS

TODAY'S PURCHASES

CIRCLE ONE

APPLY TRIGGER FINGERS TO ANALYSE THIS PURCHASE

5 SUPERIOR SALES MEMORY

NAME YOUR 5 MOST IMPORTANT CUSTOMERS.

6 BREATHING SPACE

7 SALES SPEAK

WORD:

Definition:

8 SALES DETECT(IVE) P p O p D

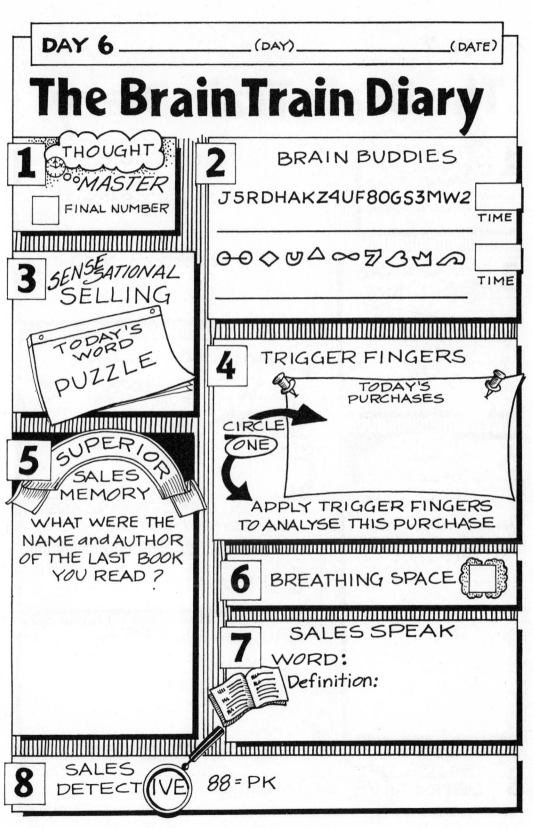

DAY 6 _____ (DAY) _____ (DATE)

The Brain Train Diary

1 THOUGHT MASTER
☐ FINAL NUMBER

2 BRAIN BUDDIES

J5RDHAKZ4UF80GS3MW2

TIME

⬡⬡◇∪△∞7ᗡᗩ⌒

TIME

3 SENSESATIONAL SELLING

TODAY'S WORD PUZZLE

4 TRIGGER FINGERS

TODAY'S PURCHASES

CIRCLE ONE

APPLY TRIGGER FINGERS TO ANALYSE THIS PURCHASE

5 SUPERIOR SALES MEMORY

WHAT WERE THE NAME and AUTHOR OF THE LAST BOOK YOU READ ?

6 BREATHING SPACE

7 SALES SPEAK
WORD:
Definition:

8 SALES DETECTIVE   88 = PK

105

The Brain Train Diary

1 THOUGHT °°MASTER

☐ FINAL NUMBER

2 BRAIN BUDDIES

J5RDHAKZ4UF80GS3MW2 ☐

TIME

⊶◇∪△∞7ɜ̃ɯ~ ☐

TIME

3 SENSÉSATIONAL SELLING

TODAY'S WORD

CAR

4 TRIGGER FINGERS

TODAY'S PURCHASES

CIRCLE ONE

APPLY TRIGGER FINGERS TO ANALYSE THIS PURCHASE

5 SUPERIOR SALES MEMORY

WHAT WERE YOU DOING YESTERDAY AT THIS TIME?

6 BREATHING SPACE ☐

7 SALES SPEAK

WORD:

Definition:

8 SALES DETECT(IVE) 8 = T on an O

The Brain Train Diary

1 THOUGHT MASTER
FINAL NUMBER

2 BRAIN BUDDIES

J5RDHAKZ4UF80GS3MW2

TIME

∞∞◇♡△∞7⌐♡♔⌒

TIME

3 SENSE SATIONAL SELLING

TODAY'S WORD
FOREST

4 TRIGGER FINGERS

TODAY'S PURCHASES

CIRCLE ONE

APPLY TRIGGER FINGERS TO ANALYSE THIS PURCHASE

5 SUPERIOR SALES MEMORY

WHAT KIND of THINGS DO YOU HAVE A GOOD MEMORY FOR?

6 BREATHING SPACE

7 SALES SPEAK
WORD:
Definition:

8 SALES DETECTIVE   26 = L in the A

The Brain Train Diary

1 THOUGHT MASTER
FINAL NUMBER

2 BRAIN BUDDIES

J5RDHAKZ4UF8OGS3MW2

TIME

⊶ ◇ ∪ △ ∞ 7 ᗺ ꝏ ᷤ

TIME

3 SENSE SATIONAL SELLING

TODAY'S WORD
HOUSE

4 TRIGGER FINGERS

TODAY'S PURCHASES

CIRCLE ONE

APPLY TRIGGER FINGERS
TO ANALYSE THIS PURCHASE

5 SUPERIOR SALES MEMORY

NAME AS MANY PEOPLE AS YOU CAN FROM YOUR LAST YEAR OF SCHOOL.

6 BREATHING SPACE

7 SALES SPEAK
WORD:
Definition:

8 SALES DETECTIVE SIGHT LOVE
SIGHT
SIGHT

108

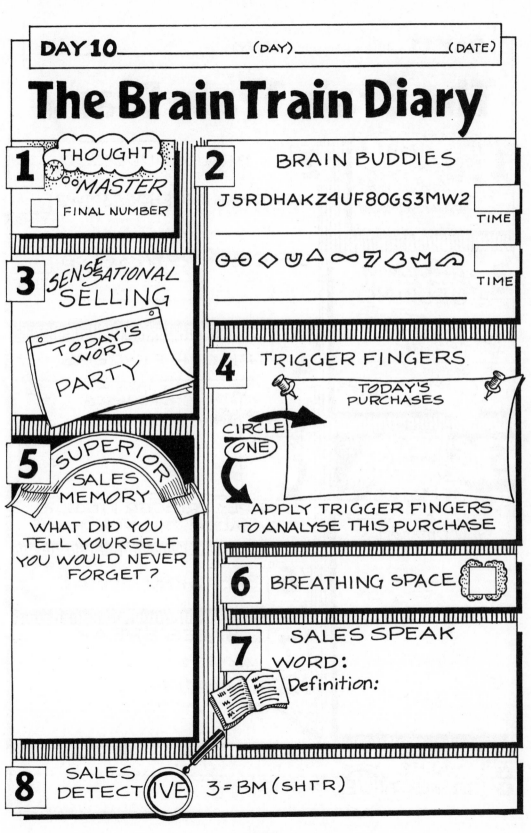

The Brain Train Diary

1 THOUGHT MASTER

FINAL NUMBER

2 BRAIN BUDDIES

J5RDHAKZ4UF80GS3MW2

TIME

TIME

3 SENSE SATIONAL SELLING

TODAY'S WORD

CINEMA

4 TRIGGER FINGERS

TODAY'S PURCHASES

CIRCLE ONE

APPLY TRIGGER FINGERS TO ANALYSE THIS PURCHASE

5 SUPERIOR SALES MEMORY

LIST 10 THINGS YOU DID TODAY.

6 BREATHING SPACE

7 SALES SPEAK

WORD:

Definition:

8 SALES DETECTIVE SEA-SONS

The Brain Train Diary

1 THOUGHT °°MASTER

☐ FINAL NUMBER

2 BRAIN BUDDIES

J5RDHAKZ4UF8OGS3MW2

TIME

⊙─⊙ ◇ ʊ △ ∞ 7 ᗷ ᗝ ᓚ

TIME

3 SENSESATIONAL SELLING

TODAY'S WORD

ICE CREAM

4 TRIGGER FINGERS

TODAY'S PURCHASES

CIRCLE ONE

APPLY TRIGGER FINGERS TO ANALYSE THIS PURCHASE

5 SUPERIOR SALES MEMORY

EVER FORGET ONE OF YOUR "THINGS TO DO"? WE'LL SHOW YOU HOW TO REMEMBER BY USING THE MEMORY PEG SYSTEM. START BY MEMORIZING THE 1ST 5 PEGS.

ONE IS BUN
TWO IS SWAN
THREE IS HEART
FOUR IS YACHT
FIVE IS HOOK

6 BREATHING SPACE

7 SALES SPEAK

WORD:

Definition:

8 SALES DETECTIVE 24 = H in a D

The Brain Train Diary

1 THOUGHT MASTER

☐ FINAL NUMBER

2 BRAIN BUDDIES

J5RDHAKZ4UF80GS3MW2

_____ [TIME]

∞ ◇ ♡ △ ∞ 7 ⌐ ⌐ ⌐

_____ [TIME]

3 SENSESATIONAL SELLING

TODAY'S WORD

AEROPLANE

4 TRIGGER FINGERS

TODAY'S PURCHASES

CIRCLE ONE

APPLY TRIGGER FINGERS TO ANALYSE THIS PURCHASE

5 SUPERIOR SALES MEMORY

NAME 5 COMPETITORS OR THE NAMES OF THEIR PRODUCTS/SERVICES

6 BREATHING SPACE

7 SALES SPEAK

WORD:
Definition:

8 SALES DETECTIVE VAD ERS

The Brain Train Diary

1 THOUGHT MASTER
☐ FINAL NUMBER

2 BRAIN BUDDIES

J5RDHAKZ4UF80GS3MW2 ☐ TIME

⚬⚬◇♡△∾7ᗡ♡⌒ ☐ TIME

3 SENSESATIONAL SELLING

TODAY'S WORD
RAIN

4 TRIGGER FINGERS

TODAY'S PURCHASES

CIRCLE ONE

APPLY TRIGGER FINGERS TO ANALYSE THIS PURCHASE

5 SUPERIOR SALES MEMORY

WHAT WERE YOU THINKING OF HALF AN HOUR AGO?

6 BREATHING SPACE

7 SALES SPEAK
WORD:
Definition:

8 SALES DETECTIVE 4 = D in a PC

The Brain Train Diary

1 THOUGHT MASTER

☐ FINAL NUMBER

2 BRAIN BUDDIES

J5RDHAKZ4UF8OGS3MW2

TIME

TIME

3 SENSE SATIONAL SELLING

TODAY'S WORD
WEDDING

4 TRIGGER FINGERS

TODAY'S PURCHASES

CIRCLE ONE

APPLY TRIGGER FINGERS TO ANALYSE THIS PURCHASE

5 SUPERIOR SALES MEMORY

NAME THE PERSON IN HISTORY YOU MOST RESPECT.

6 BREATHING SPACE

7 SALES SPEAK

WORD:
Definition:

8 SALES DETECTIVE 57 = HV

The Brain Train Diary

1 THOUGHT MASTER
FINAL NUMBER

2 BRAIN BUDDIES

J5RDHAKZ4UF8OGS3MW2

TIME

∞⟲◇⌣△∞7⌐♡⌒

TIME

3 SENSESATIONAL SELLING

TODAY'S WORD
SUPERMARKET

4 TRIGGER FINGERS

TODAY'S PURCHASES

CIRCLE ONE

APPLY TRIGGER FINGERS
TO ANALYSE THIS PURCHASE

5 SUPERIOR SALES MEMORY

MEMORIZE THE FOLLOWING LIST OF PEG WORDS.

SIX IS ELEPHANT'S TRUNK
SEVEN IS CLIFF
EIGHT IS SNOWMAN
NINE IS BALLOON and STICK
TEN IS BAT and BALL

6 BREATHING SPACE

7 SALES SPEAK
WORD:
Definition:

8 SALES DETECTIVE $AP = 1000W$

115

The BrainTrain Diary

1 THOUGHT MASTER

FINAL NUMBER

2 BRAIN BUDDIES

J5RDHAKZ4UF80GS3MW2

TIME

⊙—⊙ ◇ ∪△ ∞ 7 ᴈᴗ ᴂ

TIME

3 SENSESATIONAL SELLING

TODAY'S WORD
POST OFFICE

4 TRIGGER FINGERS

TODAY'S PURCHASES

CIRCLE ONE

APPLY TRIGGER FINGERS TO ANALYSE THIS PURCHASE

5 SUPERIOR SALES MEMORY

NAME 10 FOODS THAT YOU LIKE.

6 BREATHING SPACE

7 SALES SPEAK

WORD:

Definition:

8 SALES DETECTIVE 29 = D in Fina LY

The Brain Train Diary

1 THOUGHT MASTER
☐ FINAL NUMBER

2 BRAIN BUDDIES

J5RDHAKZ4UF8OGS3MW2 ☐ TIME

⟁⟁◇ᴗ△∞7ᘓ◡◠ ☐ TIME

3 SENSEsATIONAL SELLING

TODAY'S WORD
DRY CLEANER

4 TRIGGER FINGERS
TODAY'S PURCHASES

CIRCLE ONE

APPLY TRIGGER FINGERS TO ANALYSE THIS PURCHASE

5 SUPERIOR SALES MEMORY

NAME 12 STREETS IN YOUR NEIGHBOURHOOD.

6 BREATHING SPACE ☐

7 SALES SPEAK
WORD:
Definition:

8 SALES DETECT(IVE) 64 = S on a CB

The Brain Train Diary

1 THOUGHT MASTER
☐ FINAL NUMBER

2 BRAIN BUDDIES

J5RDHAKZ4UF80GS3MW2

TIME

⊶⊶ ◇ ♡ △ ∞ 7 3 ♡ ⌒

TIME

3 SENSE SATIONAL SELLING

TODAY'S WORD
RAILWAY STATION

4 TRIGGER FINGERS

TODAY'S PURCHASES

CIRCLE ONE

APPLY TRIGGER FINGERS TO ANALYSE THIS PURCHASE

5 SUPERIOR SALES MEMORY

NAME 5 PROSPECTS YOU ARE PLANNING TO CONTACT

6 BREATHING SPACE

7 SALES SPEAK
WORD:
Definition:

8 SALES DETECTIVE 40 D and N of the GF

The Brain Train Diary

1 THOUGHT MASTER

☐ FINAL NUMBER

2 BRAIN BUDDIES

J5RDHAKZ4UF80GS3MW2

TIME

⊶ ◇ ♡ △ ∞ 7 ♡ ♔ ∽

TIME

3 SENSE SATIONAL SELLING

TODAY'S WORD
WINTER'S DAY

4 TRIGGER FINGERS

TODAY'S PURCHASES

CIRCLE ONE

APPLY TRIGGER FINGERS TO ANALYSE THIS PURCHASE

5 SUPERIOR SALES MEMORY

WITHOUT LOOKING BACK, LIST ALL 10 PEG WORDS FROM DAYS 12 and 16.

6 BREATHING SPACE

7 SALES SPEAK

WORD:
Definition:

8 SALES DETECTIVE   15 = Mon a DMC

The Brain Train Diary

1 THOUGHT °°MASTER

☐ FINAL NUMBER

2 BRAIN BUDDIES

J5RDHAKZ4UF80GS3MW2

_____
TIME

∞−○◇∪△∞フ♄♡⌒

TIME

3 SENSÉSATIONAL SELLING

TODAY'S WORD
WARM BATH

4 TRIGGER FINGERS

TODAY'S PURCHASES

CIRCLE ONE

APPLY TRIGGER FINGERS TO ANALYSE THIS PURCHASE

5 SUPERIOR SALES MEMORY

NAME ALL THE COUNTRIES YOU HAVE VISITED IN THE LAST 5 YEARS.

6 BREATHING SPACE

7 SALES SPEAK

WORD:
Definition:

8 SALES DETECTIVE

CLOSE
CLOSE
CLOSE
CLOSE

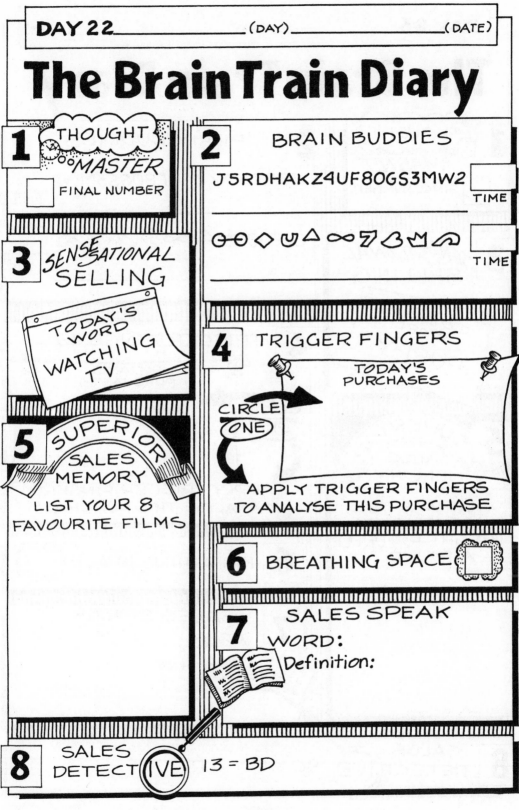

The Brain Train Diary

DAY 22 _____ (DAY) _____ (DATE)

1 THOUGHT MASTER
☐ FINAL NUMBER

2 BRAIN BUDDIES

J5RDHAKZ4UF80GS3MW2
TIME

⊙∞ ◇ ♡△ ∞7 ౮౧ TIME

3 SENSE SATIONAL SELLING
TODAY'S WORD
WATCHING TV

4 TRIGGER FINGERS
TODAY'S PURCHASES
CIRCLE ONE
APPLY TRIGGER FINGERS TO ANALYSE THIS PURCHASE

5 SUPERIOR SALES MEMORY
LIST YOUR 8 FAVOURITE FILMS

6 BREATHING SPACE

7 SALES SPEAK
WORD:
Definition:

8 SALES DETECTIVE   13 = BD

The Brain Train Diary

1 THOUGHT MASTER
☐ FINAL NUMBER

2 BRAIN BUDDIES

J5RDHAKZ4UF80GS3MW2 ☐ TIME

⌾o ◇ ⌣ ⌢ △ ∞ 7 ʒ ⌣ ↶ ☐ TIME

3 SENSE SATIONAL SELLING

TODAY'S WORD
PUPPY

4 TRIGGER FINGERS
TODAY'S PURCHASES

CIRCLE ONE

APPLY TRIGGER FINGERS TO ANALYSE THIS PURCHASE

5 SUPERIOR SALES MEMORY

WHAT WAS THE LAST ITEM YOU BOUGHT FOR UNDER A POUND?

6 BREATHING SPACE ☐

7 SALES SPEAK
WORD:
Definition:

8 SALES DETECTIVE   90 = D in a RA

The Brain Train Diary

1 THOUGHT MASTER
FINAL NUMBER

2 BRAIN BUDDIES

J5RDHAKZ4UF80GS3MW2

TIME

∞∞◇♡△∞7ꝛꙭ⌒

TIME

3 SENSE SATIONAL SELLING

TODAY'S WORD
POLICE STATION

4 TRIGGER FINGERS

TODAY'S PURCHASES

CIRCLE ONE

APPLY TRIGGER FINGERS TO ANALYSE THIS PURCHASE

5 SUPERIOR SALES MEMORY

THINK OF 10 ITEMS YOU COULD BUY FROM YOUR SUPERMARKET AND THEN LINK THEM TO YOUR 10 MENTAL PEGS.

EXAMPLE

6 BREATHING SPACE

7 SALES SPEAK
WORD:
Definition:

8 SALES DETECT IVE   24 = BBB in a P

The Brain Train Diary

1 THOUGHT MASTER
☐ FINAL NUMBER

2 BRAIN BUDDIES

J5RDHAKZ4UF80GS3MW2

TIME

∞⟳◇◡△∝7☽ᗧ⌒

TIME

3 SENSESATIONAL SELLING

TODAY'S WORD
SNOW

4 TRIGGER FINGERS

TODAY'S PURCHASES

CIRCLE ONE

APPLY TRIGGER FINGERS TO ANALYSE THIS PURCHASE

5 SUPERIOR SALES MEMORY

USING YOUR MEMORY PEGS, WRITE DOWN THE 10 SUPERMARKET ITEMS YOU DECIDED ON YESTERDAY, WITHOUT LOOKING BACK.

6 BREATHING SPACE

7 SALES SPEAK

WORD:
Definition:

8 SALES DETECTIVE   54 = C in a P (WITH THE Js)

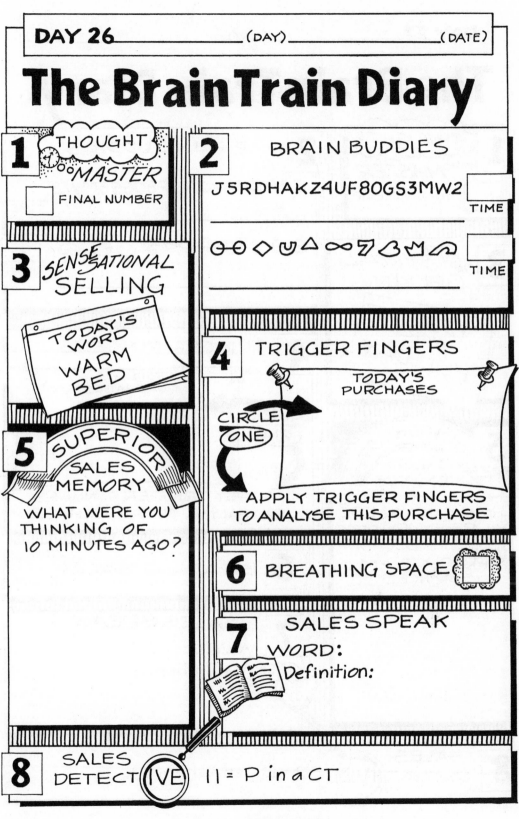

DAY 26 _____ (DAY) _____ (DATE)

The Brain Train Diary

1 THOUGHT MASTER
☐ FINAL NUMBER

2 BRAIN BUDDIES

J5RDHAKZ4UF80GS3MW2
_____ TIME

⚬⚬ ◇ ʊ△ ∞ 7 ȝ ᴄ ⌒
_____ TIME

3 SENSESATIONAL SELLING

TODAY'S WORD
WARM BED

4 TRIGGER FINGERS
TODAY'S PURCHASES

CIRCLE ONE

APPLY TRIGGER FINGERS TO ANALYSE THIS PURCHASE

5 SUPERIOR SALES MEMORY

WHAT WERE YOU THINKING OF 10 MINUTES AGO?

6 BREATHING SPACE

7 SALES SPEAK
WORD:
Definition:

8 SALES DETECTIVE 11 = P in a CT

The Brain Train Diary

1 THOUGHT MASTER
☐ FINAL NUMBER

2 BRAIN BUDDIES

J5RDHAKZ4UF8OGS3MW2

TIME

◦—◦ ◇ ∪ △ ∞ 7 ? ♡

TIME

3 SENSESATIONAL SELLING

TODAY'S WORD

HOLIDAY

4 TRIGGER FINGERS

TODAY'S PURCHASES

CIRCLE ONE

APPLY TRIGGER FINGERS TO ANALYSE THIS PURCHASE

5 SUPERIOR SALES MEMORY

HOW CAN YOU USE YOUR MEMORY PEGS TO REMEMBER YOUR PRODUCTS and SERVICES?

6 BREATHING SPACE

7 SALES SPEAK
WORD:
Definition:

8 SALES DETECTIVE   32 = DF at which WF

The Brain Train Diary

1 THOUGHT °°MASTER

FINAL NUMBER

2 BRAIN BUDDIES

J5RDHAKZ4UF80GS3MW2

TIME

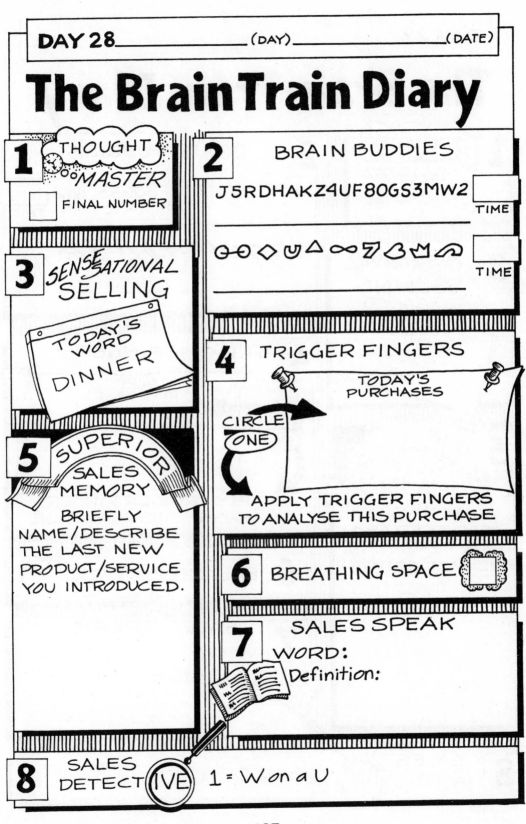

TIME

3 SENSESATIONAL SELLING

TODAY'S WORD

DINNER

4 TRIGGER FINGERS

TODAY'S PURCHASES

CIRCLE ONE

APPLY TRIGGER FINGERS TO ANALYSE THIS PURCHASE

5 SUPERIOR SALES MEMORY

BRIEFLY NAME/DESCRIBE THE LAST NEW PRODUCT/SERVICE YOU INTRODUCED.

6 BREATHING SPACE

7 SALES SPEAK

WORD:

Definition:

8 SALES DETECT(IVE)   1 = W on a U

The Brain Train Diary

1 THOUGHT °°°MASTER
☐ FINAL NUMBER

2 BRAIN BUDDIES

J5RDHAKZ4UF8OGS3MW2

TIME

⌀⌀ ◇ ♡ △ ∞ 7 ろ ㄓ ∼

TIME

3 SENSE SATIONAL SELLING

TODAY'S WORD
CLEAN HOUSE

4 TRIGGER FINGERS

TODAY'S PURCHASES

CIRCLE ONE

APPLY TRIGGER FINGERS TO ANALYSE THIS PURCHASE

5 SUPERIOR SALES MEMORY

WHAT HAVE YOU DISCOVERED ABOUT YOUR MEMORY IN THE LAST 28 DAYS?

6 BREATHING SPACE

7 SALES SPEAK
WORD:
Definition:

8 SALES DETECT(IVE) 200 = P for PG in M

128

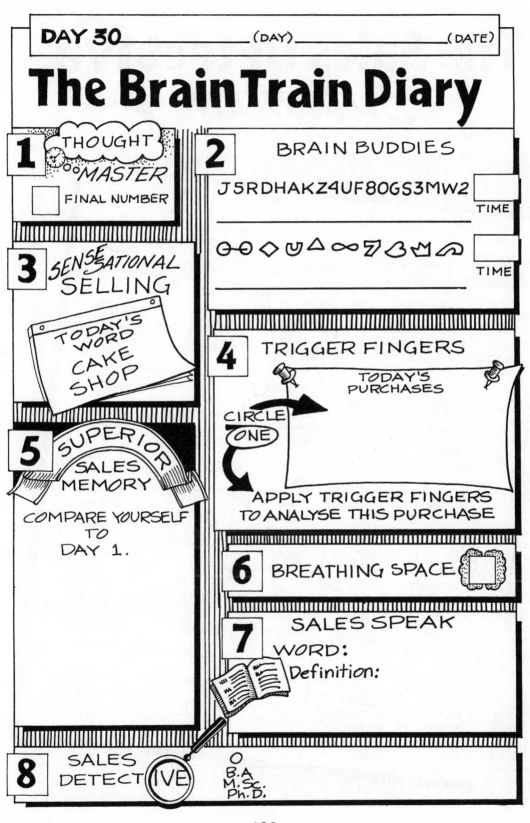

DAY 30 _____ (DAY) _____ (DATE)

The Brain Train Diary

1 THOUGHT MASTER
☐ FINAL NUMBER

2 BRAIN BUDDIES

J5RDHAKZ4UF80GS3MW2 | TIME

⊶◇♡△∞7ᗱᗷᗣ | TIME

3 SENSE SATIONAL SELLING

TODAY'S WORD
CAKE SHOP

4 TRIGGER FINGERS

TODAY'S PURCHASES

CIRCLE ONE

APPLY TRIGGER FINGERS TO ANALYSE THIS PURCHASE

5 SUPERIOR SALES MEMORY

COMPARE YOURSELF TO DAY 1.

6 BREATHING SPACE

7 SALES SPEAK
WORD:
Definition:

8 SALES DETECT(IVE)
O
B.A
M.Sc.
Ph.D.

The Sales Detective
Calendar

1 7 WONDERS OF THE WORLD	**2** 1001 ARABIAN NIGHTS	**3** 12 SIGNS OF THE ZODIAC	**4** 9 PLANETS IN THE SOLAR SYSTEM	**5** 2 PEAS IN A POD
6 88 PIANO KEYS	**7** 8 TENTACLES ON AN OCTOPUS	**8** 26 LETTERS IN THE ALPHABET	**9** LOVE AT FIRST SIGHT	**10** 3 BLIND MICE (SEE HOW THEY RUN)
11 IN BETWEEN SEASONS	**12** 24 HOURS IN A DAY	**13** SPACE INVADERS	**14** 4 DOORS IN A PASSENGER CAR	**15** 57 HEINZ VARIETIES
16 A PICTURE IS WORTH 1,000 WORDS	**17** 29 DAYS IN FEBRUARY IN A LEAP YEAR	**18** 64 SPACES ON A CHESS BOARD	**19** 40 DAYS AND NIGHTS OF THE GREAT FLOOD	**20** 15 MEN ON A DEAD MAN'S CHEST
21 FORECLOSE	**22** 13 IN A BAKER'S DOZEN	**23** 90 DEGREES IN A RIGHT ANGLE	**24** 24 BLACKBIRDS BAKED IN A PIE	**25** 54 CARDS IN A PACK (WITH THE JOKERS)
26 11 PLAYERS IN A CRICKET TEAM	**27** 32 DEGREES FAHRENHEIT AT WHICH WATER FREEZES	**28** 1 WHEEL ON A UNICYCLE	**29** 200 POUNDS FOR PASSING GO IN MONOPOLY	**30** 3 DEGREES BELOW ZERO

PROGRESS *and* PERSONAL
Observations

MIND MAP and RECORD
YOUR
PROGRESS and PERSONAL
OBSERVATIONS

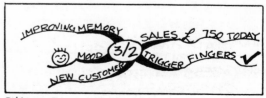

EXAMPLE

PROGRESS and PERSONAL
Observations

MIND MAP and RECORD
YOUR
PROGRESS and PERSONAL
OBSERVATIONS

PROGRESS and PERSONAL
Observations

PROGRESS _and_ PERSONAL
Observations

PROGRESS and PERSONAL
Observations

MIND MAP and RECORD
YOUR
PROGRESS and PERSONAL
OBSERVATIONS

135